Gold of El Dorado

From the exhibition GOLD OF EL DORADO: The Heritage of Colombia

Text by Warwick Bray, Institute of Archaeology, University of London

Featuring photographs by Lee Boltin

Preface by Thomas D. Nicholson, Director, American Museum of Natural History

American Museum of Natural History/Harry N. Abrams, Inc., Publishers, New York

Gold of El Dorado

Gold of El Dorado: The Heritage of Colombia is exhibited at the American Museum of Natural History, New York; the Field Museum of Natural History, Chicago; the California Academy of Science, San Francisco; and the New Orleans Museum of Art, New Orleans.

Gold of El Dorado: The Heritage of Colombia is sponsored by the Chemical Bank. The national tour of the exhibition has also received generous support from the National Endowment for the Humanities and from the National Endowment for the Arts (Arts and Artifacts Indemnity Program).

Editorial Supervision

For American Museum of Natural History:
Alan Ternes
Pat Rotter

For Harry N. Abrams, Inc.:
Nai Y. Chang
Robert Morton
Joanne Greenspun
Gilda Kuhlman

Library of Congress Cataloging in Publication Data
Bray, Warwick.
 Gold of El Dorado.
  1. Indians of South America—Colombia—Goldwork—
Exhibitions. 2. Banco de la República, Bogotá. Museo
del Oro—Exhibitions. I. Boltin, Lee. II. Title.
F2270.1.G57B7   739.2′2   79-17247
ISBN 0-8109-2224-X
Library of Congress Catalog Card Number: 79-17247
Illustrations © 1979 American Museum of Natural History
Published in 1979 by Harry N. Abrams, Incorporated, New York
All rights reserved. No part of the contents of this book may be
reproduced without the written permission of the publishers
Printed and bound in Japan

Preface

The idea for *Gold of El Dorado: The Heritage of Colombia,* the exhibition and the book, began more than three years ago with the imagination and foresight of Robert G. Goelet, President of the American Museum of Natural History. Mr. Goelet is a person of broad experience and long memory. His business and personal contacts in Colombia led him to suggest the potential for relationships between the Museum and the institutions of that fascinating South American country, and he offered to help initiate and nurture them. When the Museum administration proposed the possibility of exhibiting a loan collection from the famous Museo del Oro of Bogotá, Mr. Goelet made the contacts and gave valuable assistance in approaching the right offices.

From there, it was still a long road to the exhibition that opened in New York in November, 1979, and that was the stimulus for this book. Most important in the initial negotiations were the cooperation and encouragement of the managers and staff of the Museo del Oro and its parent institution, the Banco de la República. We are especially grateful to Dr. Germán Botera de los Ríos, Director General of the bank, to Dr. Luis Duque Gómez, Director of the Museo del Oro, and to Dr. Alec Bright, Dra. Ana María Falchetti de Sáenz, and Sra. Clemencia Plazas de Nieto of the museum staff. From the time of their warm and enthusiastic responses to our earliest inquiries, they have been unfailingly helpful.

Most of the gold objects in the exhibition and illustrated in this book are from the outstanding collections of the Museo del Oro. The sensitive and beautiful display of its collections in the impressive new museum building in Bogotá has inspired much of the organization in *Gold of El Dorado: The Heritage of Colombia.* We hope that the United States exhibition and this book will motivate many to see the collection and exhibition in the Museo del Oro itself, a truly unforgettable experience.

Gold of El Dorado: The Heritage of Colombia is about objects beautiful, rare, and precious that tell the story of the Americas before Europeans came, and of the explorations, discoveries, and changes that resulted from foreign contact. Through the golden artifacts, we glimpse the prosperous and talented peoples that inhabited the rich land of Colombia for many centuries, the turmoil that followed European contact, and the ambitions and motives of the adventurers who conquered half a continent in search of their treasure. The collection in the exhibition is the most comprehensive and varied ever seen outside Colombia. It includes more than five hundred objects of gold, supplemented with other artifacts that help us understand the use and significance of the objects and the technology that produced them. They represent all the major gold styles from the region that is now Colombia, and they illustrate the full range of the goldworking skills and arts.

While the Museo del Oro is the principal contributor to *Gold of*

El Dorado: The Heritage of Colombia, the exhibition includes important additions from other museums and from private collections in Bogotá and elsewhere. These loans have significantly strengthened the diversity of gold styles, technology, and uses represented in the United States exhibition. In particular, we acknowledge the cooperation of the Museo Nacional and the Museo Arqueológico of Banco Popular, both in Bogotá; the British Museum, the Museum of Mankind, the Cambridge University Museum of Archaeology and Anthropology, and the Institute of Archaeology, London University, in England; the Museo de América, Madrid; and the University Museum, the University of Pennsylvania, and the Field Museum of Natural History in the United States. Among private sources, we are grateful to the Galería Cano, Alec Bright, Hernán Borrero Urrutia, and Jaime Errázuriz for their loans and advice, and for other assistance.

In Bogotá, we have had splendid support from Dra. Gloria Zea de Uribe, Vice Minister of Culture, whose enthusiasm for her country and its heritage was an important factor in our success with the exhibition. We are also grateful to Dr. Alvaro Soto Holquín, Director, and Dra. Lucía de Perdomo, of the Museo Nacional, and to Dr. Pedro Restrepo Peláez, Director of the Museo Arqueológico of Banco Popular. Sr. Guillermo Cano Mejía of Galería Cano has been helpful in other ways as well, besides lending specimens.

We have also been assisted by many colleagues in London, in particular Sir Hugh Casson, President of the Royal Academy of Arts (where the exhibition was shown in London), Peter Saabor of Carlton Cleeve, Limited (organizer of the London show), Dr. Warwick Bray of the University of London (curator of the London show and author of the text in this book), Malcolm McLeod, Keeper, Ethnography Department, and Elizabeth Carmichael, Keeper of the South American Collection, at the Museum of Mankind, British Museum. Dr. Peter Munro, Director of the Kestner-Museum, Hanover, Germany, was most generous in allowing us to photograph specimens of the collection. The Hon. José Luis Rosello, Deputy Consul, and Dr. D. Carlos Martínez Barbeito, Director, the Spanish Consulate, New York, and Dra. Mercedes Palao Iglesias of the Museo de América were most helpful in arranging the loan from that museum, as was Dr. D. Evelio Verdera, Director General of Artistic Patrimony, Archives and Museums of the Ministry of Culture in Spain. We also acknowledge the skill and dedication of Lee Boltin in taking for us many of the photographs used in illustrating this book, and of Alan Ternes, Editor of *Natural History* magazine, in arranging for the publication of *Gold of El Dorado: The Heritage of Colombia.*

Thomas D. Nicholson, *Director,*
American Museum of Natural History, New York

right: *The Golden Man. Engraving by Theodor de Bry, from* Historia Americae, *published in Frankfurt, 1590.*

left, above: *Lake Guatavita; the first published illustration, from Humboldt and Bonpland's* Vue des Cordillères, *1810.*

left, below: *Lake Guatavita, showing the Sepúlveda cut.*

Gold of El Dorado: The Heritage of Colombia

The Legend of El Dorado

The Spaniards had been in Colombia for over thirty years and they had found gold, though not enough to feed their greed. Then, in 1539, when the first Spanish expeditions reached the Muisca kingdoms of the distant interior, the Conquistadors began to hear rumors of El Dorado, the Gilded Man, and the golden ritual offerings thrown into the sacred, deep blue lake of Guatavita.

He went about all covered with powdered gold, as casually as if it were powdered salt. For it seemed to him that to wear any other finery was less beautiful, and that to put on ornaments or arms made of gold worked by hammering, stamping, or any other means was a vulgar and common thing.—*Gonzalo Fernández de Oviedo, 1535–48*

The Muisca Indians told of a ceremony performed on the appointment of a new ruler:

They stripped the heir to his skin, and anointed him with a sticky earth on which they placed gold dust so that he was completely covered with this metal. They placed him on a raft...and at his feet they placed a great heap of gold and emeralds for him to offer to his god. On the raft with him went four principal subject chiefs, decked in plumes, crowns, bracelets, pendants, and earrings all of gold. They, too, were naked, and each one carried his offering. As the raft left the shore the music began, with trumpets, flutes, and other instruments, and with singing which shook the mountains and valleys, until, when the raft reached the center of the lagoon, they raised a banner as a signal for silence.

The gilded Indian then made his offering, throwing out all the pile of gold into the middle of the lake, and the chiefs who had accompanied him did the same on their own accounts.

After this they lowered the flag, which had remained up during the whole time of offering, and, as the raft moved toward the shore, the shouting began again, with pipes, flutes, and large teams of singers and dancers. With this ceremony the new ruler was received, and was recognized as lord and king. From this ceremony came the celebrated name of El Dorado which has cost so many lives.—*Juan Rodríguez Freyle, 1636*

Reports of the Guatavita treasure continued to reach the Spaniards from all sides. The ruler of the town of Simijaca attested that, in the days of his predecessor, he had personally accompanied a caravan of forty Indians, loaded with gold, which they threw into the lake. Other local chiefs had also sent offerings, and, in corroboration of these stories, the Spaniards themselves had found a few gold items in the shallows. Having robbed the living Indians of most of their gold, it was time to attack the richest treasure of all.

About 1545, an attempt to drain the lake was made by Hernán Pérez de Quesada. During the dry season he formed a bucket chain of laborers with gourd jars, and after three months' work managed to lower the water level by about three meters—enough to expose the edges of the lake bed, though not its center. According to contemporary accounts, he obtained between three and four thousand pesos of gold (a peso equals .146 ounces).

Many unknown Spaniards tried their luck with Guatavita, some of them with success. The most serious of the recorded attempts was made by Antonio de Sepúlveda, a rich merchant of Santa Fe de Bogotá. In the 1580s he began operations on a large scale. Using eight thousand Indian workmen, he cut a great notch in the rim of the lake through which some of the water ran out, lowering the level by twenty meters before the cut collapsed, killing many of the laborers and causing the abandonment of the scheme.

The best epitaph for Sepúlveda (apart from his cut, which is still a prominent feature of the landscape) comes from one of his old friends:

He said that, from the part of the lake margin that he managed to uncover, he obtained more than 12,000 pesos. Much later, the desire came over him to make another attempt at drainage, but he could not, and in the end he died poor and tired. I knew him well, and I helped to bury him in the church at Guatavita.—*Juan Rodríguez Freyle, 1636*

In 1801, Alexander von Humboldt, the foremost natural scientist of his day, spent two months in Bogotá, during which he visited Guatavita, where he commented on Sepúlveda's cut and measured the heights of the mountains overlooking the lake.

Back home in Paris after his travels, Humboldt tried to calculate how much gold the lake might contain. Estimating that one thousand pilgrims might have visited Guatavita each year, over a period of one hundred years, and that each visitor threw in five objects, he arrived at the figure of about five hundred thousand offerings, worth (in 1807) some thirty million dollars.

From that century to this one, men have invented schemes to drain Lake Guatavita and uncover its riches. Although the central zone of the lake remains untouched, many of these teams had partial success and picked up a few more gold items to add to the spoils, until in 1965 the Colombian government brought Guatavita under legal protection as part of the nation's historical and cultural heritage.

The Regions of Gold

The world map of 1529 did nothing to dispel the fantasies of gold-hungry Europeans, for in 1513–14 Ferdinand II had changed the name of this new land from Tierra Firme (the mainland) to Castilla del Oro (Golden Castile). (It was not until much later that it was called after Columbus.) El Dorado was the myth, but what lay beyond that myth was an unknown land of complex geographical features ranging from lush rain forests to snow-capped mountains, from arid deserts to grass-rich savannas and fog-shrouded valleys.

From the Caribbean to the Pacific, the invaders met diverse tribes of Indians speaking many different languages. Some tribes fought them ferociously, others joined with them in their battles, and some led them to gold. What the Spaniards were not given, they took. They scoured the land obsessively for gold. A few wrote chronicles, filled with facts about the land and its native inhabitants. Historians and, for the past century, archaeologists have woven together some of the threads of these lost civilizations. We are now beginning to understand the different tribal art styles, and the archaeology of the gold-working regions.

The Indians were buried with as much wealth as possible, and so they strove with the utmost diligence throughout their lives to acquire and amass all the gold they could, which they took from their own land and were buried with it, believing that the more metal they carried away with them the more esteemed they would be in the places and regions to which they imagined their souls would go.—*Pedro de Cieza de León, 1554*

In the sixteenth century, the Spaniards explored the lagoons and savannas of the Sinú region of northwest Colombia, one of the richest and most populous areas of the northern coast. When Pedro de Heredia visited its principal town in 1534, he found very large communal or multifamily houses, each of which was surrounded by smaller buildings for servants and stores. In a corner of the main square was a temple big enough to hold more than a thousand people, and containing twenty-four wooden idols covered with sheet gold. These images were arranged in pairs, each pair supporting a hammock filled with golden offerings. Around the temple were the burial mounds of chiefs, each mound topped by a tree whose branches were hung with golden bells.

One of the most interesting recent discoveries is a circular burial mound typical of Sinú chiefs, at El Japón, on the east bank of the Rio San Jorge. It covered two skeletons, each resting on a sloping stone slab. In the space below these slabs, offerings were deposited: a piece of cloth, a creature carved from shell, a double-spouted container made of stone, a mirror of black volcanic glass, several pots, flat and cylindrical terra-cotta stamps, and many gold pieces—breastplates, bracelets, a crown, beads, nose ornaments, bells, and ear ornaments of false filigree.

The most distinctive Sinú pieces are the staff heads, of unknown use, surmounted by figures of human beings, animals, or big-beaked birds. Some of the finest

Sinú goldwork is executed in the false filigree technique, seen at its best in matching sets of fan-shaped ear ornaments.

The mountainous Tairona lands and the adjacent Caribbean coast were densely populated, and it was not until about 1600 (after a series of native rebellions) that the last of the Tairona groups submitted to Spanish rule. Ancient Tairona settlements range from villages of no more than thirty houses to large towns with a thousand or more dwellings spread over an area of several hectares. These Indians also constructed irrigation canals and agricultural terraces for maize and a variety of other crops, and their skill as engineers and architects is attested by the stone roads, reservoirs, bridges, and stairways which are widespread in former Tairona territory.

There were ceremonial houses much larger than the ordinary dwellings. One of these contained caches of ritual stone objects buried in pots or underneath stone slabs. Beside the entrance was a jaguar skull. Even today all the ceremonial houses of the Kogi Indians, descendants of the prehistoric Taironas, are dedicated to Cashindúcua, the jaguar god.

There was a small-scale trade in gold objects between the Sierra Nevada and the Sinú, but the main commercial links were with the Muiscas, to whom the Taironas sent gold nose ornaments, beads, and seashells in return for emeralds. The Taironas often portrayed pugnacious warrior figures on their pendants.

In Spanish chronicles the Muisca (or Chibcha) kingdoms of the high, temperate plateaus of Cundinamarca and Boyacá are described in enthusiastic terms. The land was fertile, with numerous towns of wood-and-thatch huts surrounded by palisades. The individual towns were organized into two loose confederations, controlled by two chieftains, one from the south and one from the north.

Religion centered on the cult of the sun, though offerings were made to a multitude of other deities. At Sogamoso there was a large wooden temple, but caves, hilltops, woods, and lakes were also considered sacred places. The five holy lakes (Guatavita, Guasca, Siecha, Teusacá, and Ubaque) were inhabited by snake gods, and became pilgrimage centers. At all these places, idols were set up and offerings were made.

...the image of a person, completely hollow, made of pottery and ill-proportioned, open at the top, in which they put golden jewels, animals, and figures. They closed the opening with a lid, also of clay...And, when these were full, they buried them in a sacred place.—*Juan de Castellanos, 1589*

The Quimbaya region, in the Cauca Valley of central Colombia, was the homeland of many different tribes in the sixteenth century, only one of them called the Quimbaya. These tribes often spoke mutually unintelligible languages, but despite regional and local differences, all shared certain customs. The Indians were farmers who lived in wood-and-thatch houses in villages under the control of chiefs; they were rich in gold, worshiped idols made of wood or wax, and had sha-

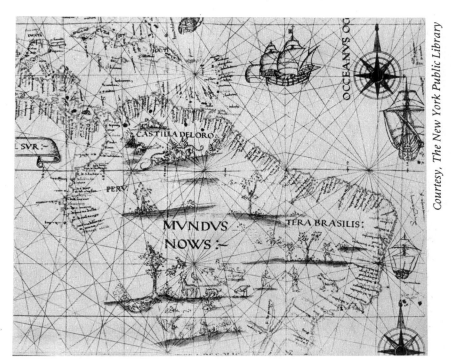

A detail of Diogo Ribeiro's ''Universal Chart'' of 1529, showing the northern section of South America, and, in particular detail, the Caribbean and Pacific coasts of Colombia—labeled ''Castillo del Oro'' (Golden Castille).

A more detailed map of South America by Levinus Hulsius, from Voyages, published in Nuremberg in 1599.

mans who communicated with the gods. They were also given to drinking bouts, and were warlike and cannibalistic. After a series of elaborate rituals, the dead were buried in deep shaft graves:

When their chiefs die in a part of this province called Tauya, they place their bodies in hammocks and light fires all round. Holes are dug beneath, into which the melted fat drops, and when the body is half burned the relatives come and make great lamentations, drinking their wine and reciting songs of praise to

Courtesy, American Museum of Natural History

Indians killing themselves and their children rather than submitting to servitude under the Conquistadors. From History of the New World *by Girolamo Benzoni, 1541–56. First translated into English and published in London in 1857.*

Cannibalistic tribesmen pouring molten gold down the throat of a Spanish captive, and butchering and roasting the flesh of another. From Girolamo Benzoni.

Courtesy, American Museum of Natural History

ʾtheir gods according to their custom, and as they have been taught by their elders. This being done, they wrap the bodies in shrouds, and keep them for several years unburied. When they are thoroughly dried up, they put them into sepulchers which they make their houses.—*Pedro de Cieza de León, 1554*

Most of the Quimbaya gold comes from looted tombs. Many of the simpler items (bells, frog pendants, disks, and nose ornaments) are widespread in central Colombia and were shared by many tribes over a large area.

One group of goldwork, however, stands out from the rest and defines the Quimbaya style in its more restricted sense. These specimens are often big and heavy, superbly finished, with a preference for large plane surfaces and restrained decoration. The essential unity of the style is shown by the treatment of the human figures used to embellish lime flasks, trumpets, helmets, and ornaments. Both men and women are represented, modeled in the round, with plump bodies and small hands and feet, naked except for their jewelry. The half-closed eyes, with their heavy lids, have a sleepy or drugged expression, and some of the figures carry lime flasks and coca-chewing paraphernalia.

Though coca was not the only drug used by the Indians, it was probably the most common. Not a hallucinogen but a simple narcotic, coca was used mainly to assuage hunger and thirst. The Indians—then and now—carried the leaves in a bag. A small lime flask, also called a *poporo*, held the crushed shell or lime. A small quantity of lime on a dipper would be passed across the lips to mix with the chewed coca leaves, and the alkaline base it created would help the absorption of the cocaine. The use of coca was mostly secular, but it also plays a part in ritual and religious ceremonies. Its ability to keep the user awake and to clear the mind helped the Indians in their nightlong religious and philosophical discussions. Today's lime flasks are made from gourds, not gold, and the lime dippers are sticks.

The modern district of Tolima, in the middle Magdalena Valley, was the home of two distinct Indian groups. In the northern portion lived the Panches, a tribe of bellicose headhunters, of whom Pedro Simón wrote: "They were such ferocious people, and such great butchers of human flesh, that they did not know how to exist without continuous wars against their neighbors—not to expand their territory and kingdom, which is the usual reason for going to war, but to obtain human flesh to eat." Their permanent enemies were the Muiscas, with whom they alternately fought and traded, exchanging the gold of Ibagué for the salt, emeralds, and cotton mantles of the highlands.

Their neighbors in southern Tolima were the Pijao Indians, who had a similar reputation as warriors and cannibals, but were also skilled goldsmiths. Most of the goldwork of southern Tolima comes from looted cemeteries, and lacks background information. The most characteristic objects are flat, stylized human figures, terminating in crescent-shaped bases.

Both men and women have their noses pierced, and wear a sort of twisted nail in them, of gold about the thickness of a finger, called *cariauris*. They also wear necklaces of fine gold, beautifully worked, and earrings of twisted gold.—*Pedro de Cieza de León, 1554*

In the twentieth century, the upper Calima Valley, in the western Cordillera of the Andes, became famous for its rich graves. Wherever recent colonists have cleared the forests, traces of ancient occupation have been revealed in the form of rock carvings, house platforms, shaft tombs, ridged fields in the valley bottom, and mosaics of little square fields on the slopes.

The gold objects found in the Calima shaft tombs are masterpieces of hammering and casting. Ear spools, nose ornaments, masks, lime flasks, and pectorals were made from sheet metal, with human faces in high relief—all of them further decorated with repoussé designs and dangling elements. Characteristically, these items are large and made of relatively pure gold.

Photograph by George Holton, from Photo Researchers

A shaft tomb with a San Agustín stone sculpture.

In contrast, the finest cast pieces—pins or lime dippers topped with birds, human figures, and imaginary animals—are miniatures. Since all the material comes from illegal excavations, its precise age is unknown, though there are hints that it may be some of the oldest goldwork in Colombia.

In the Popayán region, the usual shaft tombs and house platforms are reported as well as a few isolated stone statues of nude male figures with hands folded over the stomach. Metalwork from the tombs consists of copper and gold disks, and a series of pendants in which human features are combined with those of eagles or birds of prey.

The main theme of San Agustín sculpture is a human or semihuman personage, sometimes partly transformed into a jaguar with bared fangs, or else with a jaguar-monster crouching over his back and head. With the aid of hallucinatory snuffs and drug-induced visions, present-day shamans communicate with the spirits and can transform themselves into jaguars and other animals. Although details of costume and weapons are realistically depicted, the sculpture of San Agustín belongs more to this spirit world than to the world of everyday life. Surprisingly little gold has come from San Agustín, though the site has produced evidence of metalworking in about the first century A.D.

The finest underground tombs of Tierradentro consist of a spiral stairway leading to a roughly circular, subterranean chamber with niches round the sides, and a roof supported by columns of natural rock. Walls and roofs were sometimes painted in black, white, red, and yellow with geometric designs, stylized human faces, and lizard-like creatures.

When they die, they make the tombs very large and very deep…And among them it is the custom, as they informed me, that, if one of their lords dies, each of the neighbors round about gives the dead man two or three Indian men and women. They take them to the place of burial and there give these Indians much maize wine, so much that they become drunk. And, seeing them without feeling, they put these people into the tomb to keep the dead man company.—*Pedro de Cieza de León, on the Quillacingas, 1554*

Stone monolith at San Agustín showing a monster crouching atop a human figure.

At the time of the Conquest, the highland Nariño area, near Ecuador, was the homeland of the Pasto and Quillacinga Indians. Identical archaeological material is found also on the Ecuadorian side of the frontier.

Many Nariño tombs contain shells traded from the Pacific Coast. Another item of trade was coca. Pottery figures of coca-chewers are typical, but the leaf must have been imported from the warmer regions to the west, for at the time of European contact the tropical Pacific lowlands supplied the Pasto merchants with gold, cotton, shell beads, and coca leaf.

The goldwork of Nariño forms a distinctive body of material, whose stylistic links are with Ecuador and the central Andes. Many pieces have a pale color, indicating an alloy with a good deal of silver. Characteristic are the matching pairs of ear disks with repoussé patterns and the ornaments decorated with cutout monkeys. From the later period come the finest nose ornaments of sheet metal, some of them bicolored or bimetallic pieces.

Before we, the negroes, arrived, the Indians lived here, in this same place. The Indians lived under the ground, and ate gold from golden plates and drank gold from golden cups, and their children played with dolls made of gold. When we arrived the Indians fled, under the earth toward the mountains where the rivers have their sources...But before fleeing, the Indians took all the gold, the cups full of golden pineapples and the golden dolls, and broke everything up with their hands and feet, turning it all into gold dust...And now we, the negroes, must break our bodies to find the gold dust and to keep ourselves alive in the places where the Indians used to live before.—*myth of the miners of Güelmambi, Barbacoas; from Nina S. de Friedemann,* Minería, Descendencia y Orfebrería Artesanal Litoral Pacifico, Colombia, *Bogotá, 1974*

The coastal strip just north of Ecuador, called the Tumaco region, was first explored in 1526–27 by the ships of Francisco Pizarro, on his way to the conquest of Peru. The Pacific province was described as populous and rich:

They wear short shirts which do not cover their shameful parts, and they are tonsured like friars, except that they cut all their hair in front and behind, but let it grow at the sides. They wear emeralds and other things in their nostrils and ears, and strings of gold, turquoises, white and colored stones.—*Francisco López de Gómara, on the Esmeraldas, 1552*

Archaeological sites have yielded a rich haul to treasure hunters, who wash and sieve the earth in search of little studs, nose rings, and tiny gold ornaments which are the stock-in-trade of the Tumaco jeweler.

The Art of the Goldsmith

The goldsmiths of Dabeiba, Guatavita, and other gold-working centers were masters of a subtle and demanding art, and their products were in no way primitive. Though the Spaniards ignored artistic quality, preferring their gold in ingot form, the occasional piece sent back to Europe was marveled at by goldsmiths and artists for its aesthetic and technical qualities. As Albrecht Dürer, one of Europe's greatest artists, wrote in 1520, after his first glimpse of native American goldwork: "I never in all my days saw anything that so delighted my heart as these things. For I saw amazing objects, and I marveled at the subtle ingenuity of the men in these distant lands." And Benvenuto Cellini, when shown a piece of gold from Mexico, attempted to copy it and found he couldn't.

Within the Americas, the knowledge of metal technology spread from south to north. The first use of beaten gold is dated about 2000 B.C. at the site of Waywaka in the Andes of southern Peru, after which there was a long period of purely local Peruvian development, with new techniques introduced into the repertoire from time to time. By contrast, metallurgy did not reach Mexico until some time between A.D. 700 and 900, and it arrived fully developed, without any preceding stage of experimentation.

Colombia, Panama, and Costa Rica can be regarded

as a single metallurgical province, characterized by a preference for gold-copper alloys, lost-wax casting, depletion gilding, and false filigree. Within this area, gold objects were traded in both directions. Tairona, Sinú, and Quimbaya pieces have been found in tombs as far north as Panama and Costa Rica and were imitated locally; Colombian emeralds were incorporated in Panamanian gold jewelry at Coclé; and Panamanian frog pendants have been found as far south as Armenia in the Quimbaya region of Colombia.

In spite of the vast number of extant specimens, the classification and dating of Colombian goldwork still offer problems, though there are certain definite criteria. The presence of European trade goods (for example, iron tools and glass beads) in the same tombs as the gold is proof that certain styles were current when the Spaniards arrived. These styles can be placed within a late period. Some metalwork, clearly older, like the finest Quimbaya pieces, belongs to a middle period of development, dated around the fifth to ninth centuries A.D. Metalwork of the early period, around the time of Christ, is represented by objects in the Early Calima style. Few of these objects were excavated by trained archaeologists, and most of the museum pieces were obtained from collectors or treasure hunters who had little interest in the context of their finds. Except in rare instances, they did not record which items were found together in the same tomb, did not save the pottery (which is often our best guide for dating), and did not collect such "valueless" materials as charcoal, which, since the 1950s, has been used to provide radiocarbon dates for archaeological sites.

Other problems derive from the nature of the gold objects themselves. Being small, portable, and valuable, they were traded over long distances; in addition, the goldsmiths themselves were mobile, working in areas away from their homelands. As a consequence, provenance alone is not a reliable basis for classification. Pieces made in one part of Colombia turned up in another, were copied by local goldsmiths, and provided the stimulus for new, hybrid versions of the local forms.

Gold is what gave them breath;
For gold they lived, and for gold they died.
—*Juan de Castellanos, on the miners of Buriticá, 1589*

Most of the gold used by the Indians was obtained from placer mines in the rivers of the western and central Cordilleras, employing only the simplest equipment: fire-hardened digging sticks to break up the earth, and shallow wooden trays (bateas) in which to carry and wash it.

They take the earth, little by little, from the mine to the washing place, and there they clean it with water to see if there is gold in the bateas... And to wash this earth and work the mine, they do thus: they put certain Indians inside the mine to dig out the earth... and with this excavated earth they fill up bateas, which other Indians carry to the water, in which are those who do the panning, both men and women. The carriers empty their bateas into other, larger ones which those who are washing have in their hands. And the porters return for more earth while the washers pan what has already been brought... It is worth noting that each pair of Indians who wash must be served by two persons to bring the earth, and two more who excavate it and break it up to fill the carrying trays.—*Gonzalo Fernández de Oviedo, 1535–48*

Oviedo also notes that streams were sometimes diverted to expose the gold-bearing gravels of their beds. Using similar methods in the last century, it took only six to eight minutes to process a twenty-pound load of gravel.

In pre-Hispanic times, as at present, small-scale mining may have been a part-time occupation, carried out during the dry season when stream beds were exposed. Some localities, however, supported specialist communities of full-time miners and smiths. The most renowned site of this kind was Buriticá, in the mountains of northern Antioquia.

Buriticá was a true industrial center, exploiting both alluvial and vein gold, and exchanging the surplus for food and other necessities. It was a town of big houses, set close together on a fortified hilltop, and it seems to have been the capital of an area containing several other mining and metal-processing communities.

Indians panning gold from an open mine near a river. From La Historia General y Natural de la Indias *by Gonzalo Fernández de Oviedo, 1535–48.*

At Buriticá itself, and in the surrounding villages, the Conquistadors found workshops for melting down the metal, with crucibles, braziers, and balances to weigh out the gold. The general impression is that Buriticá exported both finished items and raw metal to be worked up elsewhere. Some gold and jewelry was exported to the Quimbaya and Muisca peoples but most of it was traded northward to Dabeiba, where a community of specialist goldsmiths grew up on the basis of imported raw material.

Since Colombia lacks tin, it was unable to develop a native tradition of bronzeworking. Instead, the favorite material was *tumbaga* (a gold-copper alloy with some accidental silver). Tumbaga offers several technical advantages. It is easier to cast than any of its constituent metals alone, and it reproduces fine decorative detail more accurately. The melting point is lower than that of pure gold, and the alloy harder than its individual constituents.

In the Archive of the Indies in Seville is a document, dated 1555, which describes how the Indians of Tamalameque, in lowland Colombia, melted their gold:

And then the said chief and Indians burned a little charcoal on some baked clay with three cane blowpipes, and placed a crucible on this with a piece of caricoli…along with small quantities of low grade gold…After it had melted, they took the crucible and poured a little water over it.—*on Tamalameque; from Archivo General de Indias, Seville, 1555*

Hammering was used to stretch and planish the flat parts of certain cast pieces, to make simple disks, plaques, or nose ornaments, and as a technique for producing sheet metal.

Spanish chronicles describe the use of hammers and cylindrical anvils made of hard, fine-grained stone. These hammerstones were not hafted, but were held in the hand, and the metal was worked by alternate hammering and annealing into a thin and even sheet.

A rough depiction of a method of melting and hammering gold alloy and objects. From History of the New World *by Girolamo Benzoni.*

Annealing was an essential part of the process. Pure gold is soft and fairly easy to beat, but under continual hammering many of the alloys become strain-hardened and difficult to work, finally turning brittle and cracking. Malleability can be restored by annealing—replacing the object in the furnace until the metal glows red, followed by quenching in water. After this, the metal can be hammered once more.

The techniques used to manufacture the objects themselves were relatively simple. An outline drawing was scribed on the sheet (sometimes with the aid of a template), and tool marks show that a narrow-bladed chisel was used to cut out the shape. For decorative effect, but also to give strength and rigidity to large objects of flimsy sheet, the metalsmiths pressed out repoussé designs, working from the back, with the object resting on a bed of some yielding material.

These repoussé designs were improved by working on the front of the piece, using a chasing tool to deepen the designs and to sharpen their edges. Additional freehand patterns were sometimes traced directly onto the metal. Raised designs were made by pressing and hammering the sheet metal over carved patterns, and the same technique was used to mass-produce sets of identical pieces, such as necklace pendants.

When many tiny elements—little balls or fine wires—are to be joined to each other or to a backplate, ordinary soldering becomes impractical. Copper-gold-silver alloys can be diffusion-welded by the application of heat, but the jewelers of Colombia and Ecuador also used an alternative method, called granulation, which is the one employed in the ancient civilizations of the Old World, and described by Pliny—though not rediscovered in Europe until some fifty years ago. A copper compound, such as copper hydroxide or acetate, is mixed with an organic glue, and the mixture is used to stick the delicate gold elements into place. Once assembled, the object is heated in the reducing (oxygen-free) atmosphere of a charcoal fire until the glue burns away and a natural gold-copper brazing alloy forms.

Complicated shapes, both hollow and solid, were normally made by the lost-wax (or cire-perdue) method, in which the goldsmith modeled the object in wax and then encased it in clay, leaving a channel to the exterior. On heating, the melted wax was poured out, and molten metal was poured in to replace it, leaving an exact metal copy of the wax original.

The manufacture of hollow pieces required an interior core of clay mixed with powdered charcoal, carved to the shape of the finished product. The goldsmith next rolled out molten beeswax into a thin sheet, which, laid over the core and pressed against it, followed the shape exactly. At this stage, the pouring channel and air vents were added in the form of wax rods. The object, assembled with peglike supports (chaplets) of green wood, was now heated in order to melt out the wax and to leave a space between the interior core and the outer casing. While the mold was still hot (so that the metal would not set before flowing

An imaginative recreation of a gold-casting process by Theodor de Bry, who never visited the Americas but relied on the reports of travelers.

to all parts of the cast), molten gold was poured in to take the place of the wax. After cooling, the outer casing was broken open to extract the metal casting, and the interior core material was removed. Because the outer casing has to be broken each time, every lost-wax casting is a unique creation.

To produce a gold finish on a tumbaga item, the alloy was treated chemically with an acid substance made from corrosive minerals or from the juice of certain plants, which removed the base metals at the surface, but left the gold untouched.

...they know very well how to gild the objects and items they make from copper and low-grade gold. And they have such ability and excellence in this, and give such a high luster to what they gild, that it looks like good gold of 23 carats or more.... They do this with a certain herb, and it is such a great secret that any goldsmith in Europe, or in any other part of Christendom, would soon become a rich man from this manner of gilding...I have seen the herb, and Indians have taught me about it, but I was never able, by flattery or in any other way, to get the secret from them.—*Gonzalo Fernández de Oviedo, 1535–48*

The Indian artisans did not simply produce works of gold for admiration. Their objects served a purpose, sometimes religious, sometimes secular. They manu-

factured tools from gold and its alloys—spatulas, chisels, axes, needles. Chiefs used bowls and spoons, hammered from gold. The Indians even formed fish-hooks out of the precious metal.

The human faces and animal figures used in body ornaments and on staff heads and musical instruments were often distorted into stylized forms. The inspired symbolism of many of these creations, whether based on myths or influenced by drugs, reflects the lives and beliefs of the pre-Hispanic tribes of gold-rich Colombia. We can appreciate the beauty of this tribal art even though we can never completely understand what it meant to those who made it.

Geography and diversity saved some of the Indians' heritage from the Spaniards. When they could, the native Americans kept their gold, which was buried in hidden tombs. Centuries later, the *guaqueros* (tomb robbers) found these golden treasures of lost cultures. The plundering is now illegal, but still many of these pieces find their way from the robbers' hands to the museums of the world, and in particular to the Gold Museum of Colombia in Bogotá, the showplace of twenty-five thousand pieces of pre-Colombian goldwork.

This, then, is their heritage—the gold of El Dorado, the gold that eluded the Spaniards.

Note: The goldwork illustrated in this book represents a wide variety of ornamental forms and has been chosen for its extraordinary beauty and craftsmanship. Unfortunately, it has not been possible to show examples from all of the gold regions discussed in the introductory text.

Pendant, male figure with headdress

Cast gold
Height 4 9/16″ (11.6 cm.)
Museo del Oro

Variants on this form are most common in the Sinú region, but they extend into the Isthmus of Central America as far north as Panama and Costa Rica. This pendant is more naturalistic than some, which have the body and tail of a fish. The diadem on this example is widely repeated on other pendants. This figure has ligatures tied around his legs and carries a staff with dangling ornaments.

Sinú breastplate

Hammered and repoussé gold
Width 20⅞" (53 cm.)
University Museum, University of Pennsylvania,
Philadelphia

Jaguars are shown attacking snakes on this breastplate with raised bosses, or protruding ornaments. The repoussé designs were usually scribed on gold sheet with a template or chisel, then pressed out from the back against a bed of some yielding material, such as sand or thick leather. The designs were then improved by using a chasing tool on the front of the piece to deepen and sharpen the forms.

The breastplate is cumbersome to wear and was probably used only on ceremonial occasions. It was recovered from a burial mound, looted in 1919, which yielded one of Colombia's richest treasure hoards. Goldwork of the Sinú style was in use at the time of Spanish contact in the sixteenth century, but may have come into fashion several hundred years before that period.

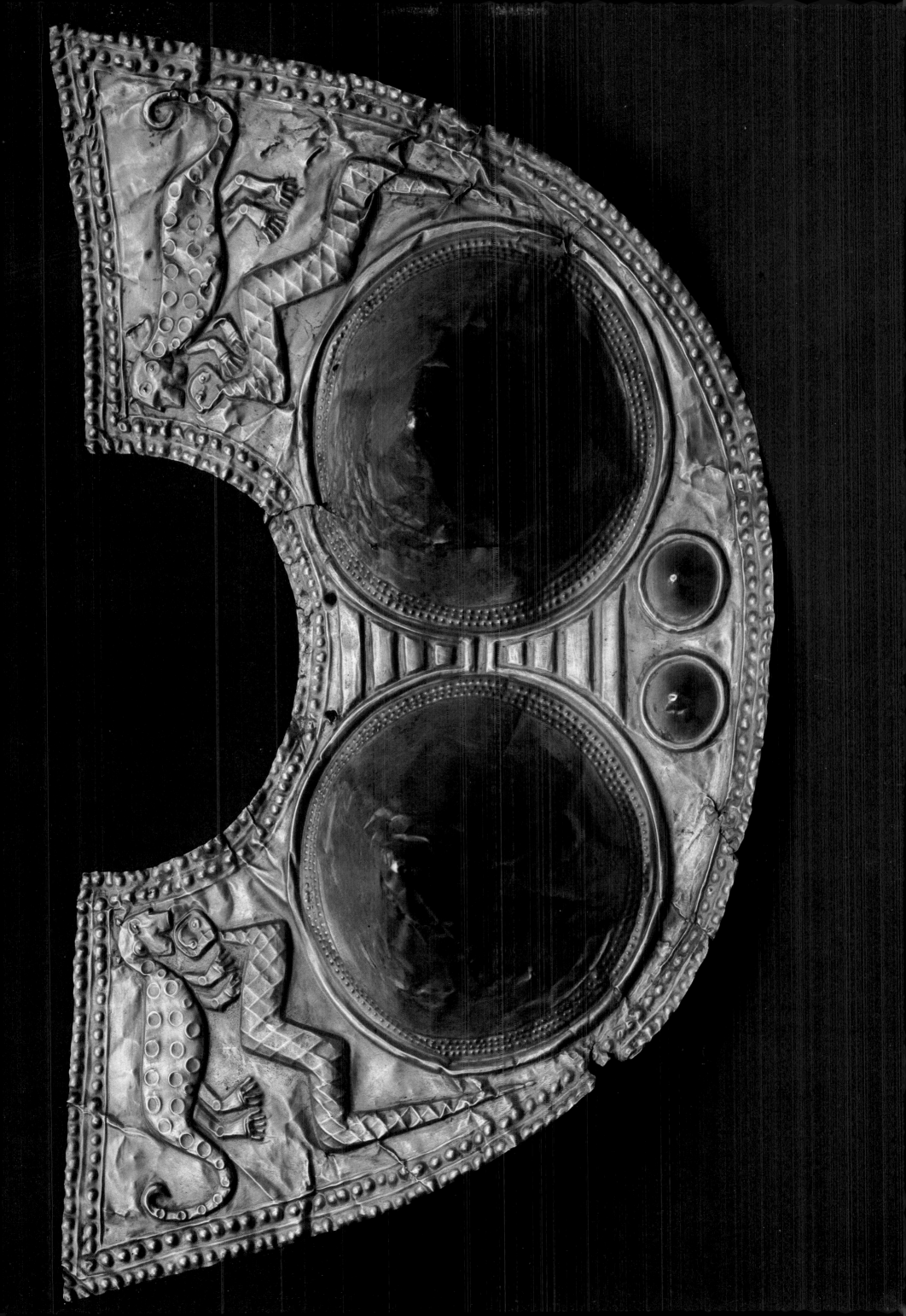

Sinú jaguar

Cast gold
El Blanco, Magdalena
Length 4 ¾" (12.1 cm.)
Museo del Oro

The jaguar remains a key figure in the mythology and religion of Indian groups all over Colombia. Under the influence of hallucinatory drugs, the shaman can turn at will into a jaguar, and in this supernatural disguise has great powers for good or evil. At death, some shamans turn permanently into jaguars, a belief recorded as early as 1625, when Pedro Simón noted that "the souls of those who die are transformed into jaguars." The jaguar may also serve as master of animals, protector of game. The Páez Indians of the Tierradentro region believe that the union between a jaguar and a woman produced a race of voracious and mischievous jaguar-spirits who attack women.

This Sinú jaguar, naturalistically represented, has loops on its front paws and may have been worn as an amulet.

Sinú false filigree ear ornaments

Animals or birds
Cast gold
San Marcos, Sucre
Width 2⅛″ (5.3 cm.)
Museo del Oro

Stylized birds

Cast gold
Guaranda, lower Cauca Valley, Bolívar
Width 2¾″ (7 cm.)
Museo del Oro

Geometric panel surmounted by stylized birds

Cast and gilt tumbaga
Colosó, Sucre
Width 2⁵/₁₆″ (5.9 cm.)
Museo del Oro

At first sight, these Sinú ear ornaments and certain nose ornaments appear to have been made by the filigree technique, in which strands of coiled and twisted wire are soldered to each other or to a backplate. However, analysis shows that most of these specimens are false filigree, not soldered at all, but cast. The model was built up from wirelike threads of wax, and the whole piece cast in a single operation by the lost-wax method.

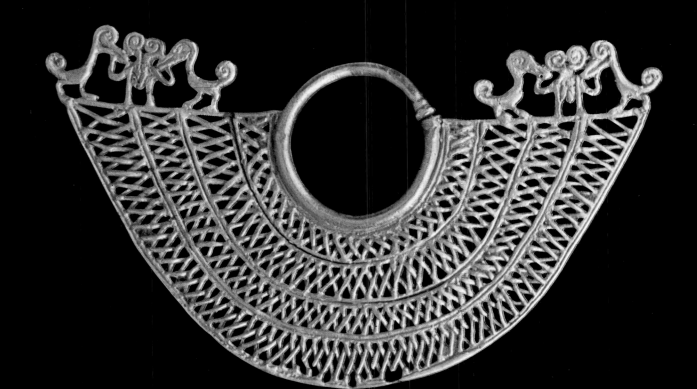

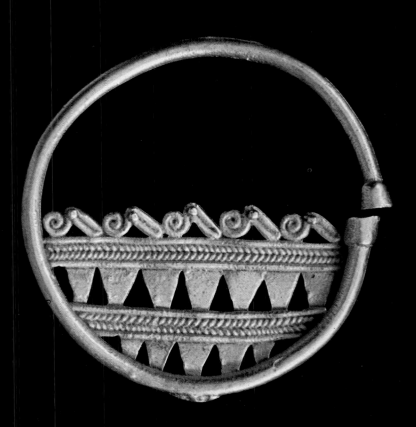

Sinú staff head, two birds

Cast gold
Ovejas, Sucre
Height 1¼" (3.1 cm.)
Museo del Oro

These objects are conventionally called staff heads, though the placement of the sockets makes it clear that most examples were attached to their shafts horizontally rather than vertically. They may possibly, therefore, have served as hooks on the ends of ceremonial spear-throwers.

The Spaniards noted that the Sinú goldsmiths made figurines of various kinds of animals and birds. The gold in which the Sinú objects were cast probably came from Buriticá or Dabeiba, further inland. Sinú gold tends to be of fine quality, with some silver but little copper.

Darien pectoral, alligator variant (left)

Cast tumbaga
Salento, Quindío
Height 2 13/16″ (7.2 cm.)
Museo del Oro

Darien pectoral (middle)

Cast gold
Height 4 9/16″ (11.6 cm.)
Museo del Oro

Darien pectoral (right)

Cast gold-rich tumbaga
Quimbaya, Quindío
Height 2 9/16″ (6.5 cm.)
Museo del Oro

The so-called Darien pectorals form an easily recognizable group within which there is a good deal of variation from very stylized forms to more naturalistic ones. The basic figure, however, is a human being, sometimes with an alligator-like head. Spiral, winged devices appear beside the face, and the headdress incorporates objects shaped like mushrooms. It has been suggested that these are representations of the Psilocybe mushroom, one of two species of hallucinogenic mushrooms that grows in Colombia. The figure may or may not wear a mask, but generally holds a pair of cylindrical objects, perhaps sticks or rattles, which often end in knobs. The legs are broad and flat, reduced almost to a plaque.

Darien pectorals were at one time thought to constitute a distinct Darien style within Colombian goldwork, but it is now clear that they are a composite of many different regional styles. The greatest concentration of finds has been in the Sinú zone, though the distribution of Darien pectorals, or closely related forms, stretches from the Tolima and Calima regions to the Caribbean coast. Pectorals of this type are also found in Panama, Costa Rica, and Yucatan, where they were most likely exported or made as local copies.

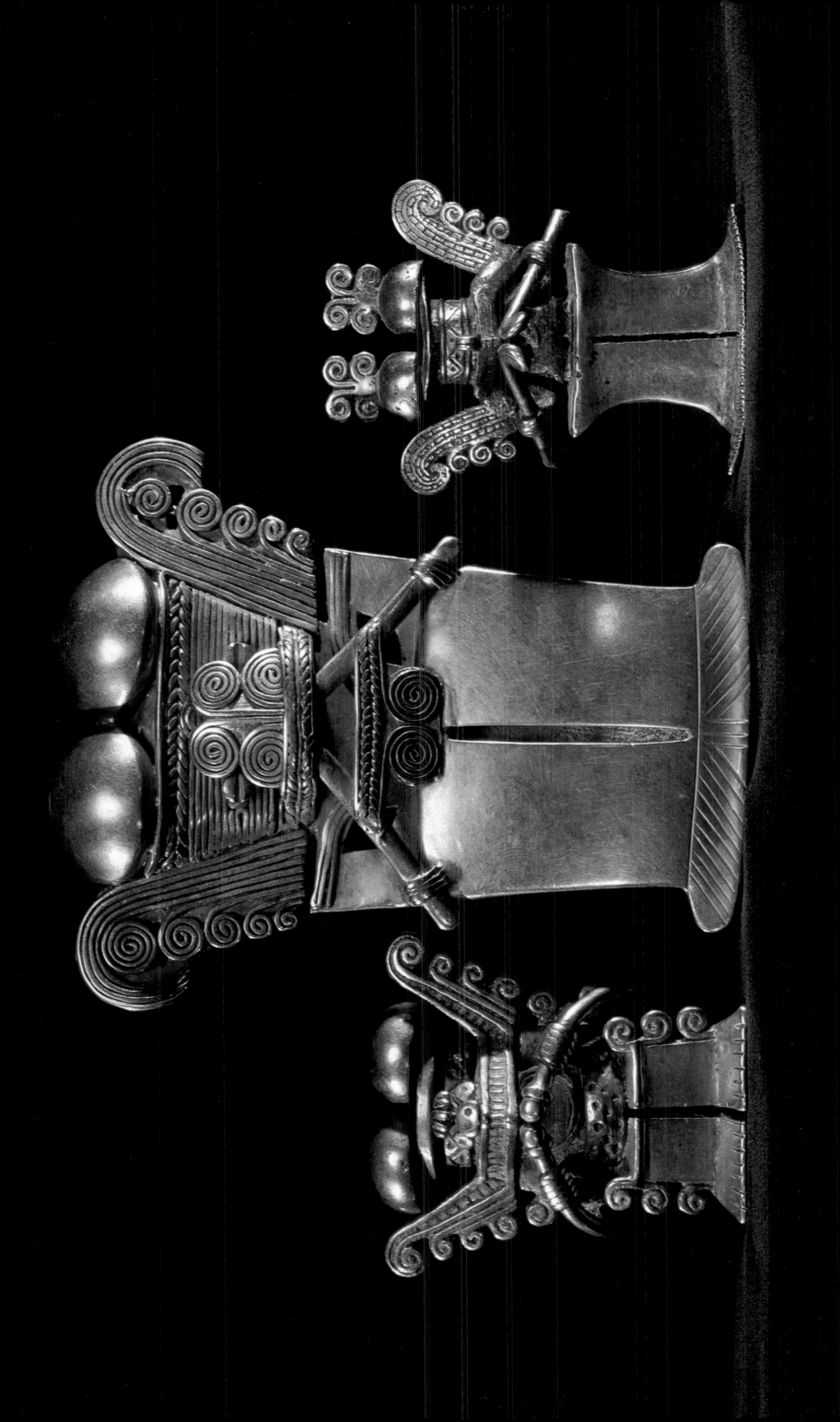

Tairona pendant

Cast and gilt tumbaga
Minca, Santa Marta, Magdalena
Height 2 ⅜″ (6.1 cm.)
Museo del Oro

The Tairona technical mastery of detail
shows itself in the geometric decorations
that outline the wings and body of this bird.
This tumbaga object has been enriched by
depletion gilding, a chemical treatment that
removed the base metals at the surface,
leaving a layer of almost pure gold. Also
called *mise-en-couleur*, this gilding was
usually accomplished with an acid solution
of macerated Oxalis plants, or with a
corrosive mineral substance which the
Mexican Indians called "gold medicine."

Tairona pendant, double-headed animal

Cast tumbaga
Bellavista, Magdalena
Length 2¾" (7.1 cm.)
Museo del Oro

This double-headed mythical beast, a composite of two animals, is a common Tairona form. Sometimes the objects are less stylized and the source animals are easier to identify. Perhaps this is one of the chimeras conceived under the influence of hallucinatory drugs. Whether inspired by the imagination, religion, or drugs, the distortions in Colombian art were deliberate, reflecting a mythology and a world view of which the details are now lost to us.

Tairona figure pendant

Cast and gilt tumbaga
San Pedro de la Sierra, Ciénaga, Magdalena
Height 4³/₁₆″ (10.6 cm.)
Museo del Oro

. . . when they went to war, they wore crowns, patens on their chests, and beautiful feathers and many other jewels . . . On their necks are very lovely necklaces of rich gold pieces, and in their ears some earrings; they pierce the septum of the nose to wear small spherical pieces of fine gold . . .
—Pedro de Cieza de León, on the Indians of central Colombia, 1554

In addition to a necklace, a diadem, a nose bar, and earrings, this Tairona figure also wears a labret (or lip plug), a penis cover, and a ferocious scowl. His headdress shows pairs of stylized birds on the front and on the side. Except for the free-hanging and typical Tairona earrings, this intricate and extravagant piece was made in a single casting.

We do not know whether the figure represents a god, a culture hero, or an actual Tairona warrior, but the ornaments he wears are faithful miniatures of types found in Tairona burial mounds.

Tairona nose ornament

Cast gold
Minca, Santa Marta, Magdalena
Width 2 ⁵/₈″ (6.6 cm.)
Museo del Oro

The clothing of the Indians of the diocese and state of Santa Marta consists of shirts and painted cotton blankets; they wear gold earrings, bits of gold in their nostrils, gold plaques and eagles on their breasts, with pebble bracelets and gold pieces on their wrists and insteps. —Vázquez de Espinosa, 1629

Nose ornaments were one of the most common forms of Indian jewelry in pre-Hispanic Colombia and ranged from simple nose plugs or rings to large, elaborately decorated pieces, some of which would have deformed the wearer's nose. This nose ornament shows the typical Tairona coils and braids, which were cast by the lost-wax method.

Muisca tunjo figure

Cast tumbaga
Height 4³/₁₆″ (10.6 cm.)
Museo del Oro

If El Dorado was, in fact, something more than a legend, it would have been objects like this, called a *tunjo*, that were thrown into the sacred lake to celebrate the accession to power of a new *cacique*, or Indian ruler. Distinctively Muisca, these tunjos were votive figures to be offered to the gods, and were not intended for everyday use. Unlike jewelry that was made for the living, these miniatures are rough and poorly finished. They are usually found buried in pots or on lake bottoms, and only rarely have they been discovered in graves or on house sites. Their purpose may have been to thank the gods for past help or to serve as gifts in anticipation of future services.

This tunjo shows a victorious warrior holding the severed head of his enemy. Spaniards reported that the Muiscas customarily took the heads of their enemies as trophies. According to Gonzalo Fernández de Oviedo, "If the men of Bogotá kill or take prisoner any Panche Indians, they take the heads back to their homeland and put them in their oratories."

The object in the figure's left hand may be a *macana*, described by Oviedo as a sword-club of polished palm wood "more or less the size of a hand in breadth, and with the edges thin and sharp. With this they used to cut, and even chop up an enemy."

Muisca tunjo on a lime dipper or pin

Cast tumbaga
Height 6 ⁵/₈″ (16.7 cm.)
The Overseas Museum, Bremen

This tunjo figure holds two children who rest in a gold basket. The basket may represent the clay pots in which the tunjos were buried.

No other Colombian art form tells us as much about the life of the common people as these tunjos, which show the Muisca people engaged in everyday activities. There are tunjo warriors holding shields and swords, or clubs, and there are hunters with quivers. One tunjo portrays a man, standing on a high platform, about to be sacrificed. Another tunjo represents a man lying on a framework of seven longitudinal poles with two crosspieces, which confirms the reports of Spanish chroniclers that the highland Muiscas slept on beds rather than in hammocks.

A typical tunjo consists of a simple plaque on which details are added in wax wire. Though the modeling is naive and one-dimensional, detail is faithfully rendered. Tunjos were usually cast head down, and occasionally they are found with the channels and funnel, into which the molten metal was poured, still in place.

Muisca shell

Cast gold
Length 3 ⅝" (9.3 cm.)
Museo del Oro

This gold shell is hollow cast, and still retains the black core material—clay and charcoal—over which it was shaped. In 1528, the merchant Pedro de Cifuentes complained about the problems of melting down native pieces. "The hollow parts are filled with an earth that is very heavy," he grumbled, "and there is little gold laid over it, so that almost half of it consists of earth, especially in the animals and birds which they make."

The inland tribes of the Muisca region traded their emeralds to the Taironas for nose ornaments, beads, and seashells made of gold. Large conch shells, sometimes covered with sheet gold, were used as trumpet-like instruments. Smaller shells, such as olive shells, were used for jewelry.

Seashells were, of course, important to the Muiscas and other Colombian peoples as a source for lime. Lime from crushed shells was chewed along with coca leaves and helped the body absorb the drug that, among other things, relieved hunger and thirst.

Muisca dragon

Cast and gilt tumbaga
El Chocho, Fusagasugá
Length $^{13}/_{16}$" (2.1 cm.)
Museum of Mankind, London

Besides the human world, Muisca tunjos
also represented the creatures that played a
part in their mythology and religion. There
were real creatures, such as the birds that
topped the forked staffs held by some tunjos,
as well as fantasy beings—dragons and
snakes, some with human faces and the ears
of animals. The Spaniard Pedro Simón tells
us something of the Muisca myths: "There
used to appear in these same waters (of Lake
Guatavita) a small dragon or large serpent,
and when it appeared they had to offer it
gold or emeralds."

Slow crystallization of the metal during the
cooling which followed the casting process
leads to the formation of dendrites, the
branched, fernlike structures which are
clearly visible on the surface of this item.

Lime container, with female figures in relief

Cast tumbaga with enriched surfaces
Filandia, Quindío
Height 11″ (28 cm.)
Museo de América, Madrid

This lime flask with a metal stopper shows a standing female figure, which is repeated on the other side. It is part of the Treasure of the Quimbayas, a cache consisting of 121 items that were found in two graves at La Soledad, Filandia, in 1891 and later presented by the Colombian government to the queen of Spain.

Two features of this object which distinguish it as Quimbaya are its elegance and its formal proportions. There are close stylistic links between Quimbaya goldwork and some of the metalwork of the early Coclé tombs in Panama of the period A.D. 500 to 800 due to trade between the two peoples. The height of the Quimbaya style falls somewhere between A.D. 400 and 1000, when the finest objects were produced.

Lime flask, seated figure

Cast tumbaga with enriched surfaces
Quimbaya style
Height 8 ¾" (22.1 cm.)
University Museum, University of
Pennsylvania, Philadelphia

This lime flask shows quite clearly how it
was made. The holes for the core supports,
used to hold the wax model and internal
core in place during casting, have been
plugged, but are still visible (on top of each
shoulder, through the upper part of each
buttock, and one at the base of the curved
sheet). The object was made in several
pieces and soldered together, while the
body and base are a single lost-wax casting.
However, in the front of the base a
rectangular hole was left through which
the core material of clay and charcoal was
removed. The upper edge of the patch that
was soldered in to cover this hole shows as
a faint line between the ankles. The figure's
forearms are of sheet metal, with traces of a
joining seam, and the feet and hands were
cast separately.

Lizard or alligator

Cast tumbaga
Length 5⅜" (13.6 cm.)
Museo del Oro

The creatures represented in Colombian goldwork were chosen for their symbolic attributes rather than for their importance as sources of food. Lizards (the terrestrial equivalents of crocodiles) figure in the mythology of several modern Indian groups, often symbolizing aspects of the mystical "creative energy" which permeates the universe and must be controlled, or properly channeled, in order to benefit mankind. Lizards, therefore, are associated with the concepts of knowledge, power, and correct social behavior.

Pectoral, two birds

Cast tumbaga
Montenegro, Quindío
Height 3½″ (9 cm.)
Museo del Oro

This relatively simple pectoral is not a
common form in the Quimbaya region.
Since similar objects have been found in the
Sinú area, we may be dealing with an item
which was imported into the Quindío from
a manufacturing center in the Caribbean
lowlands. Because of its central location
and its rich gold mines, the Quimbaya
region attracted traders from many parts of
Colombia.

Quimbaya necklace, with frogs

Hammered gold
Length of large frog 3½″ (9 cm.)
Length of tubular beads ⁹/₁₆″ (1.5 cm.)
Length of barrel beads ⅜″ (1 cm.)
Museo del Oro

The objects which compose this necklace come from two different localities and have been assembled for the purpose of exhibition. The frogs, of hammered gold, are from Pereira, Risaralda, while the twenty-three tubular beads and twenty-six barrel beads of sheet metal were found in Finca La Irlanda, Versalles, Quindío. Hammer marks are clearly visible on the large frog. The fourteen identical small ones were probably made by pressing and hammering the sheet metal over a form or template.

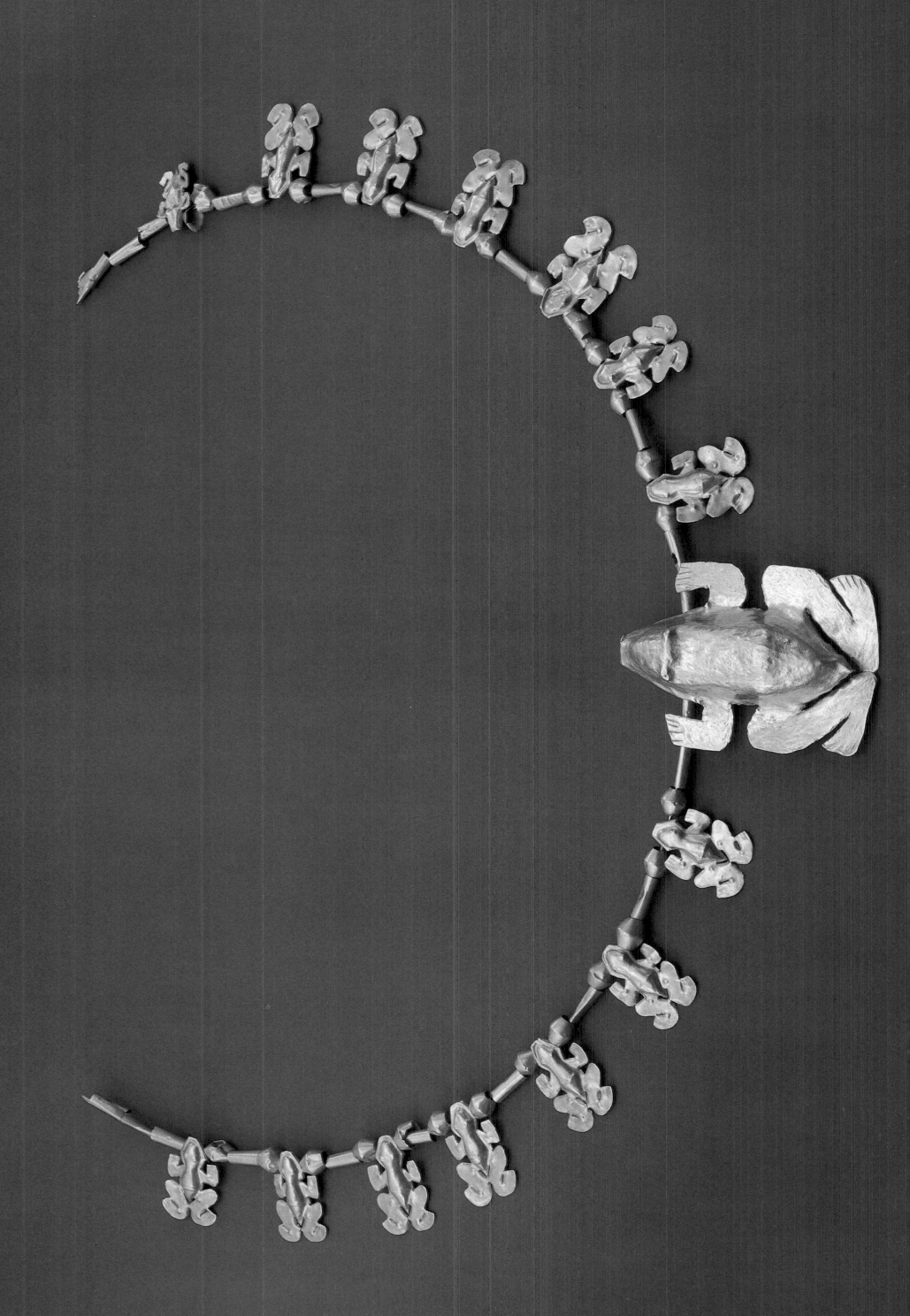

Quimbaya pectoral, human figure with dangling ornaments

Cast tumbaga
Height 4 7/8″ (12.3 cm.)
Museo del Oro

The tumbaga in this piece has a high percentage of copper, some of which has corroded to produce the green discoloration on the surface. Modern analysis confirms the sixteenth-century Spanish statements that tumbaga (also called *guanín gold*, or *caricoli*) was extremely variable in composition, often with a gold content of less than twenty percent. Even the copper-rich tumbagas could be treated so as to give a superficial appearance of pure gold, a fact which at first deceived many Spaniards. The facial features on this pectoral figure seem more realistic, less formalistic, than those of the typical Quimbaya style.

Tolima pectoral

Cast and hammered gold
Height 7 ¾" (19.7 cm.)
Museo del Oro

This Tolima pectoral has the typical
flat, stylized human figure terminating in a
crescent-shaped base.

According to unconfirmed reports from
tomb robbers that Tolima pieces have been
found in the same tombs as Quimbaya and
early Calima objects, the Tolima style must
have begun several centuries before the
Spanish conquest. In support of this view
is the fact that "dancing figures" (some
of them with long tails and sun-ray
headdresses) are a frequent theme in rock
engravings from the Quimbaya, Calima,
and Tolima regions.

Tolima tweezers

Cast and hammered gold
Chaparral, Tolima
Height 2⅝″ (6.6 cm.)
Museo del Oro

While some tweezers were devoid of decoration, these are surmounted by two birds. Others were topped with human figures or animals.

Contrary to popular belief, the presence of facial hair among Indians does not indicate an admixture of European blood. Most Indian groups, however, regarded such hair as unsightly and took pains to remove it, not by shaving (since razors were unknown) but by plucking. In 1560 Cervantes de Salazar wrote, ''The Indians of that land [Yucatan, in Mexico] were accustomed to pluck out the hair with some things like pincers, as women do their eyebrows.''

Tolima pectoral

Cast gold
Rio Blanco, Tolima
Height 7″ (17.7 cm.)
Museo del Oro

Tolima pectorals are known for their simple, abstract body shapes. Stylized birds and bats are common in Tolima metalwork. The base of this pectoral, cast by the lost-wax method, was stretched by hammering.

Trade in gold objects was widespread, bringing Calima objects into the Tolima region, and carrying Tolima pectorals to many parts of Andean Colombia from the Quimbaya zone to the San Agustín region. The distinctive, square "Tolima face" on this pectoral shows a certain overlapping of styles with other regions.

Diadem

Cut and hammered gold
Early Calima style
Height 10⅝″ (27 cm.)
Museo del Oro

The repoussé decoration on this crown is embossed from the back and chased on the front. The ear disks and a nose ornament are stapled to the central face, which seems to have been raised by hammering over a matrix.

The Early Calima style, typified by large hammered ornaments, coincides with the early period of Colombian goldwork around the time of Christ. Although the hammering of sheet metal may seem to be a more "primitive" and thus more ancient technique than casting, evidence from Colombia shows that the two techniques were introduced simultaneously.

Lime dipper surmounted by a human figure (left)

Cast gold
Restrepo, Cauca Valley
Early Calima style
Length 10 ³/₁₆″ (25.8 cm.)
Museo del Oro

Lime dippers, long pinlike objects usually surmounted by a figure, were inserted into lime flasks, and the lime or crushed shells which adhered to them was chewed with coca leaves.

Technologically, this item is a miniature *tour de force*. The figure is only one inch high but the loincloth, crown, and pendant are shown in meticulous detail, and there is a movable ring through the nose. One hand holds a transverse knife with a suspension loop while the other grasps a stafflike object with a dangling chain. Attached to the back is a funnel-shaped element with a perforated stone bead secured by a loop of twisted wire. Two concave ear disks, like the full-size examples from Calima graves, are attached at the shoulders by wire.

Lime dipper, with masked figure holding a staff (right)

Cast gold
Finca Grecia, Restrepo, Cauca Valley
From an Early Calima grave
Length 11 ¾″ (30 cm.)
Museo del Oro

This tiny figure's mask, staff, the fan-shaped object in the left hand, and the alter-ego animal figure behind the shoulders find their counterparts in the massive stone statuary in San Agustín.

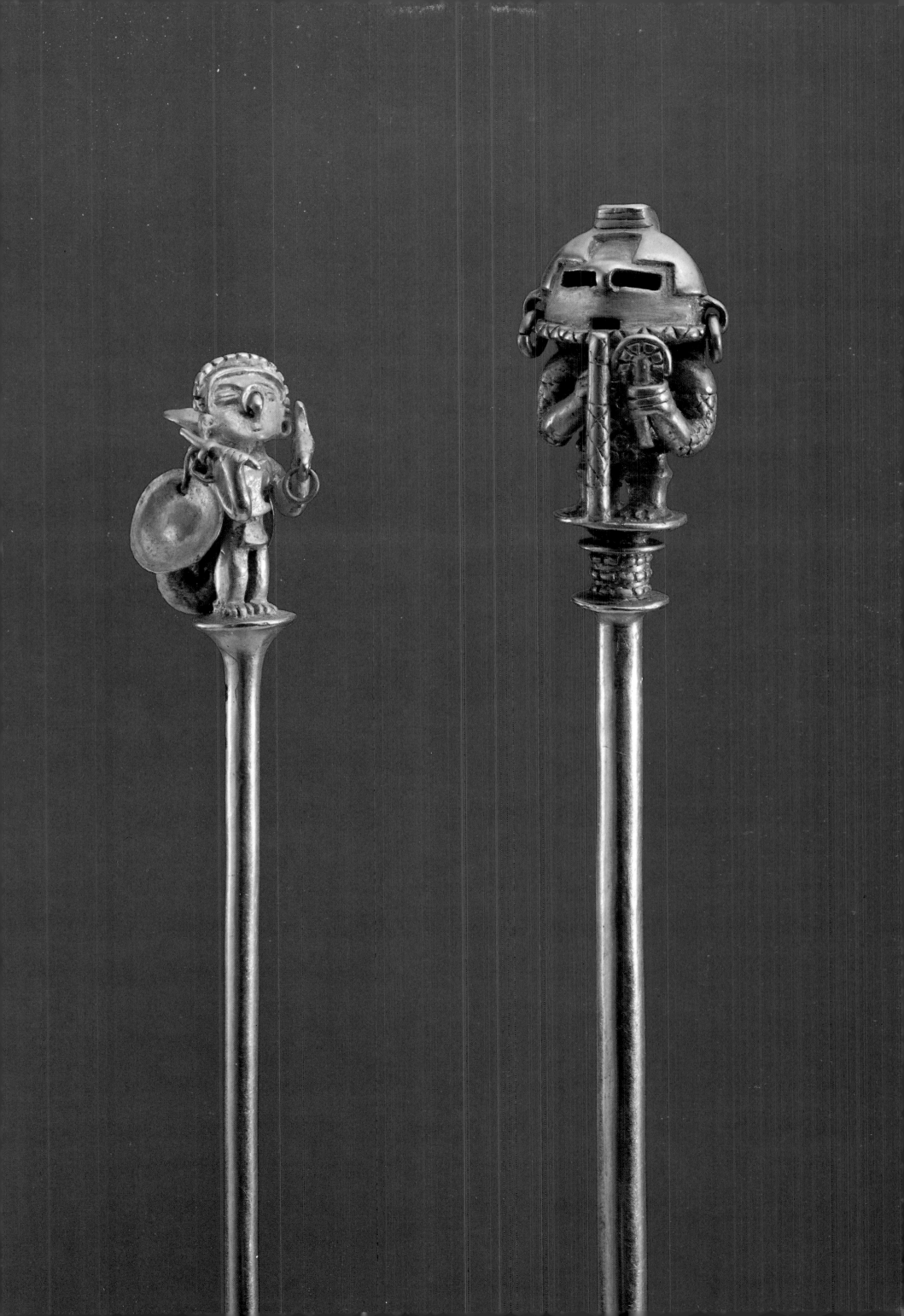

Funerary mask

Hammered gold
Restrepo, Cauca Valley
Early Calima style
Width 7⅞" (20 cm.)
Museo del Oro

A typical Calima tomb consisted of a deep
vertical shaft with a funerary chamber
opening from the bottom. The dead person
was buried with his gold jewelry, offerings
of food and drink, and everything he would
need in the afterlife. The vault was then
sealed, and the shaft filled with earth.

The features on the mask were embossed
from behind, with details touched up by
burnishing and incision on the front.

Pendant, masked figure

Cast gold
Restrepo, Cauca Valley
Height 2″ (5 cm.)
Museo del Oro

The representation of masks on gold
figurines and stone sculpture suggests
that masks played an important part in
the rituals and ceremonies of Indians in
Andean Colombia before the European
conquest, as they still do today. The face of
this mysterious figure peers out through a
large, plaquelike device extending from the
chest and around the sides of the crown. A
second, openwork mask covers the face. In
the hands are a staff, or spear, and a shield
similar to those depicted on early Calima
lime dippers. The treatment of the legs
shows the influence of Darien pendants.

Nariño ear ornaments, with jaguar faces

Hammered and repoussé gold
Pupiales, Nariño
Capulí period
Diameter 3⅜" (8.5 cm.)
Museo del Oro

The most common Nariño gold objects are breastplates, plaques for appliqués on textiles, nose ornaments, and disks, which were suspended from the ear lobes by means of wire loops. Geometric designs and stylized animal forms are the most common decorative motifs.

These ear ornaments date from the Capulí period, that is, from A.D. 800 to 1300. During this period there was clear contact with Andean cultures of Ecuador and Peru. Some of the finest objects of this period are made of sheet metal, and many pieces contain a good deal of silver.

Lime container in the form of a seated man

Cast tumbaga with enriched surfaces
Filandia, Quindío
Height 4 15/16″ (12.5 cm.)
Museo de América, Madrid

In quality and style, this lime container is a classic Quimbaya piece from the Treasure of the Quimbayas. The figure is nude except for jewelry and ligatures around the arms and legs. Suspended from the necklace is a lime flask. These containers, called *poporos*, held crushed lime and were carried by the Indians along with their bags of coca leaves. Pottery figurines from Nariño, in southern Colombia, show coca-chewers with one cheek distended by a quid of coca leaves. Today's Colombian Indians carry poporos made from gourds, for the use of gold receptacles did not survive the Spanish conquest.

Muisca pectoral, human figure

Cast gold
Chiquinquirá, Boyacá
Height 7 1/8″ (18.1 cm.)
Museo del Oro

Like many other Muisca pectorals (chest ornaments), this one has an openwork diadem, triangular fretwork, and the simple, braided motifs typical of Muisca goldwork. The head was cast from a mold made with a stone matrix, a method perfected by Muisca goldsmiths for mass-producing sets of identical cast elements for necklaces and figurine parts using the lost-wax method. Radiocarbon data suggest that the Muisca style of metalwork may have begun in the seventh century, though it was still in vogue when the Spaniards reached Bogotá some nine hundred years later.